THE IMMORTAL HERITAGE

AT TYNE COT, PASSCHENDAELE; 1922

THE IMMORTAL HERITAGE

An Account of the Work and Policy
of The Imperial War Graves Commission
during twenty years
1917–1937

by

FABIAN WARE

with an Introduction by

EDMUND BLUNDEN

and

thirty-two photographs

The Naval & Military Press Ltd

Published by

The Naval & Military Press Ltd

Unit 5 Riverside, Brambleside
Bellbrook Industrial Estate
Uckfield, East Sussex
TN22 1QQ England

Tel: +44 (0)1825 749494

www.naval-military-press.com
www.nmarchive.com

Printed and bound by CPI Group (UK) Ltd, Croydon, CR0 4YY

"TO THE
GLORY OF GOD
AND TO THE MEMORY OF
ONE MILLION DEAD
OF THE BRITISH EMPIRE
WHO FELL IN THE GREAT WAR
1914–1918

THEY DIED
IN EVERY QUARTER
OF THE EARTH AND
ON ALL ITS SEAS
AND THEIR GRAVES ARE
MADE SURE TO THEM
BY THEIR KIN

THE MAIN HOST
LIE BURIED IN THE LANDS
OF OUR ALLIES OF THE WAR
WHO HAVE SET ASIDE
THEIR RESTING PLACES
IN HONOUR
FOR EVER"

Inscription on the tablet in the Warrior's Chapel in Westminster Abbey

CONTENTS

ACKNOWLEDGEMENTS

The Imperial War Graves Commission wish to express their thanks to the following for permission to reproduce certain photographs in this book: the Imperial War Museum; the Newfoundland Government Offices; *The Times*; *Country Life*; Sport and General Press Agency; Topical Press Agency; Photopress Ltd.; Monsieur Daniel, Ypres; Mr A. Riley.

ILLUSTRATIONS

PREFATORY NOTE

On the occasion of the meeting of the Imperial Conference in London this summer, the following Memorandum was addressed to Mr Stanley Baldwin on the 23rd April by H.R.H. the Duke of Gloucester :

"In 1917, my eldest brother as Prince of Wales addressed a Minute to the Imperial War Conference enclosing a memorandum by Sir Fabian Ware, then Director-General of Graves Registration and Enquiries. In this Memorandum he proposed the creation of an Imperial Organisation to care for and maintain in perpetuity the graves of those who had fallen in the War. On the suggestion of the Prince of Wales the memorandum was submitted to the representatives of the Governments of the Empire then assembled in London for that Conference. On April 13th 1917, its terms were approved by a resolution of the Conference, and the body now known throughout the world as the Imperial War Graves Commission was thus called into being.

That was twenty years ago. In the interval a great work has been performed; and I now have the honour, as President of the Commission, to enclose a further memorandum from Sir Fabian Ware (who has been Vice-Chairman of the Commission since its foundation) in the form of a Report on what has been accomplished.

I have read this Report with keen satisfaction, and, in the belief that it will be read with equal satisfaction by the members of the coming Imperial Conference, I would invite you, as their Chairman, to commend it to their notice.

Since I assumed the Presidency of the Commission, two aspects of its work have struck me as of particular interest, quite apart from the admirable way in which, as all know, the graves are cared for. They are aspects which I think will appeal particularly to the members of the Conference.

In the first place, the Governments of the Commonwealth represented on the Commission have cooperated freely in a great piece of constructive work. Owing to their joint efforts they have produced something which has been an example to the rest of the world.

Secondly, the sympathy which has united them in honouring our dead of the Great War has not remained self-centred, but has linked them to other nations who suffered similarly on the world's battlefields, whether as our friends or as our enemies. This has led to the formation of bonds of common remembrance between former friends and foes, bonds not only of sentiment, but of a practical kind for they have led to the creation of Joint International Committees for the guardianship of the graves.

(Sgd.) HENRY

PRESIDENT

Imperial War Graves Commission"

At its Meeting on the 8th June the Conference considered the Report and Mr Neville Chamberlain, who had succeeded Mr Baldwin as Chairman, moved the following Resolution which was seconded by Mr Mackenzie King, Prime Minister of Canada, and adopted unanimously :

"The Conference considered a Memorandum from His Royal Highness the Duke of Gloucester, President of the Imperial War Graves Commission, communicating to the Conference a Report on the work of the Commission during the 20 years which have elapsed since its establishment in 1917, on the recommendation of the Imperial War Conference of that year, and decided to place on record its warm appreciation of the work which had been accomplished and of the manner in which the Commission had discharged and was continuing to discharge the duties entrusted to it.

The Conference desired that, in view of the wide interest that was taken in this work, the Imperial War Graves Commission should make arrangements for the Report to be published."

In accordance with this desire the Report is now published, slightly re-arranged and amplified, with an introduction by Mr Edmund Blunden, M.C., who has been associated with the Commission since the death of Mr Rudyard Kipling in January 1936.

F. W.

LONDON

24 July 1937

INTRODUCTION

A N ENGLISH VOICE out of the past seems sounding in my
ears as I consider the brief, unassuming, but deeply moving
history which is offered to the public in the following
pages. In the beginning of the year 1746 a young writer who had
been visiting his uncle's regiment in Flanders (it was not long
after the battle of Fontenoy) composed a classic elegy upon the
fallen. During the War of 1914–1918 that elegy by William
Collins did not go unnoticed; it was indeed recognised by many
people as an utterance appropriate to those later years and their
sacrifice also; yet it has gained in fitness and significance since then.
I take leave to transcribe it in this place, for its author might
almost be claimed as having had a prophetic sight of the cemeteries
made beautiful by the Imperial War Graves Commission:

> How sleep the Brave, who sink to Rest,
> By all their Country's Wishes blest!
> When *Spring*, with dewy Fingers cold,
> Returns to deck their hallow'd Mold,
> She there shall dress a sweeter Sod,
> Than *Fancy's* Feet have ever trod.
>
> By Fairy Hands their Knell is rung,
> By Forms unseen their Dirge is sung;
> There *Honour* comes, a Pilgrim grey,
> To bless the Turf that wraps their Clay,
> And *Freedom* shall a-while repair,
> To dwell a weeping Hermit there!

All who find opportunity to enter some of those many cemeteries,
in so many parts of the world, or even to see such pictures of them

as are contained in Mr Sydney C. Hurst's book *The Silent Cities*, or
in the present volume, must be impressed and even astonished at
the degree of beauty achieved by the creators and guardians of
these resting-places. It has been my own chance, on the old
Western Front, to witness parties of French visitors drawn to
these cemeteries by their harmonious grace and dignity of archi-
tecture, of tree, shrub, grass, and blossom; and I have heard the
effect expressed in reverent phrases. Those in particular who were
eye-witnesses of the battle-line in the World War will not yet
have forgotten scenes and circumstances which must make the work
of the Imperial War Graves Commission even more remarkable to
their judgment than it can be to the majority who were spared the
sinister realities of the modern Golgotha. In the clash and be-,
wilderment of actual fighting, in the rapid ruin and chaos and obli-
vion of the front line with its enormous process of annihilation,
perhaps not many soldiers retained the confidence that the dead—
themselves, it might be, to-morrow or the next instant—would
at length obtain some lasting and distinct memorial.

Of course the fighting man, from the earliest stages of the War,
was familiar with attempts to give proper burial to those who were
killed in action. There were well-known arrangements and orders
concerned with this sad necessity; and a great deal was done by
commanding officers and padres and the men under them in the
forward areas. "Some frail memorial" was erected duly over
many and many a grave dug under fire. But the whole problem
was vast and severe. Bombardment, which swelled month by
month into a wider extent and a fiercer violence, appeared likely
in the course of years to obliterate almost all separate burial. The
assemblies of wooden crosses in the wrecked villages near the line,
with here and there an additional sign of remembrance suggested
by the feeling and opportunity of surviving fellow-soldiers, seemed

to have a poor chance of remaining recognisable or visible after one more outburst of attack or counterblast, when high explosive and torrential steel would tear up the soil over deliberately chosen spaces of the land.

In so far as they illustrate what once seemed to be the insoluble problem of burying the dead in modern war conditions, of burying them and securing for them an honourable grave, some moments of the long ago may be recalled at this point by one of the millions of temporary soldiers. During the month of May 1915 a determined attack was launched by the British force against the German positions east of Festubert with its low, swampy, dyke-drained levels. When these operations had become old history, and the month of May had come in once again, the occupants of the Festubert breastworks could hardly dig out an old fragment of trench or disturb a crushed shelter without discovering the remains of their own countrymen or of their opponents. Hamlet and Horatio might have meditated there many a dark hour. Later that summer the battle of the Somme was fought, and men perished in great multitudes and in places where their bodies could not be recovered, so intense was the new artillery and machine-gun fire, so hopeless the mud which went on for miles. The battalions who came up to the relief of those in the craters and vestiges of trenches would find themselves, in the fire-splashed night, stumbling over corpse after corpse. In deep dug-outs, twenty or thirty feet down, friends or foes were done to death by one means or another with the ultimate result that there was no entering those burnt-out, dreadful caverns. In the following year, 1917, the battle of Passchendaele arrived with a character of its own; a still more devastating artillery fire fell upon human bodies and the dull country which (incredibly enough) had once been tilled land and thorpe; a deeper, fouler slime drowned all but the luckiest

life in man and nature. Concrete hovels, into which men crowded
with their pitiable wounds and wretched burdens, were often
struck and shattered by direct hits from heaviest artillery. At that
period above all, the soldier felt that his death would be his
complete and final disappearance. The Book of Life was for others.
He would scarcely be selected, from this grey gulf of existences
with its incessant roarings and extinctions, for any writing there.
He would pass, as the present writer has passed, the newly
shattered bodies of men like himself without the very power to be
astonished, to feel pity, to do more than mechanically register a
twisted boot by a torn rifle-butt. At that period, the idea that
these battlefields would themselves ever again become pasture-
lands, and châteaux with grounds and little lakes and garden-walls,
would have appeared sheer fantasy.

And it is true, as for example the Menin Gate and the Thiepval
Memorial testify to the moving generations, that thousands and
thousands of our dead have never yet been found; true also that to
this day, from the fields and roadsides which the farmers of France
and Belgium have made anew in the likeness of their tradition, the
bodies of some who fell in action are recovered and identified,
week upon week. The sum of the whole matter is the great design
of interment and remembrance which had taken shape so early
as 1917 and—not merely on the Western Front, but in every place
that saw the British Empire under arms—has since approached
completion. Observant readers of the chronicle of twenty years
comprised in this volume will not underestimate the complexity
of the endeavour, the devotion of the authorities, the thoroughness
of the performance implied in the main fact. It is no sufficient
comment to point out that no previous war has been marked by
anything like this fulfilment of piety towards those who gave their
lives. The battle of Waterloo was over in a day; there was no

insuperable difficulty in finding the men who had fallen, and in giving them just burial. But those who have explored the region of that extraordinary fight will know how capriciously the spirit of grateful remembrance haunted the field. The attitude of the day may be noted in the words of its Poet Laureate, writing in 1816:

> Earth had received into her silent womb
>   Her slaughtered creatures; horse and man they lay,
> And friend and foe, within the general tomb.
>   Equal had been their lot; one fatal day
> For all,..one labour,..and one place of rest
> They found within their common parent's breast.

The farmer had been busy over the land: but

> The graves he left for natural thought humane
>   Untouched; and here and there where in the strife
> Contending feet had trampled down the grain,
>   Some hardier roots were found, which of their life
> Tenacious, had put forth a second head,
> And sprung, and eared, and ripened on the dead.

> Some marks of wreck were scattered all around,
>   As shoe, and belt, and broken bandoleer,
> And hat which bore the mark of mortal wound;
>   Gun-flints and balls for those who closelier peer;
> And sometimes did the breeze upon its breath
> Bear from ill-covered graves a taint of death.

In the far-spreading labours a century later of the Imperial War Graves Commission, with which the name of Fabian Ware will always be united, a principle quite different from that of Wellington's campaigns has been evident. The ancients regarded the soldier in the mass, and felt no difficulty in consigning him accordingly without name or detail into some common sepulchre.

He was called Legion, or nothing; he was merely the means by which someone else pursued the glory of a name. It has been the faith of the Commission that those who fought and died in 1914–1918 were—what we know them to have been—several and separate personalities, each in human measure "the captain of his fate", each claiming individual comprehension. We well remember our old friends as co-operating without thought of personal advantage in the main cause. But their characterisations are clear, as various as their number; and so it is entirely laudable that the Imperial War Graves Commission has carried out its task with a vivid sense of the individual grave. This consciousness has not meant a want of coherence in the aspect of any one cemetery, nor indeed in the quality of all the many cemeteries; it has only provided the utmost range of difference possible within a general scheme of relatedness.

The beauty, the serenity, the inspiration of the Imperial cemeteries have been frequently acknowledged by more able eulogists; for my part, I venture to speak of these lovely, elegiac closes (which almost cause me to deny my own experiences in the acres they now grace) as being after all the eloquent evidence against war. Their very flowerfulness and calm tell the lingerer that the men beneath that green coverlet should be there to enjoy such influence; the tyranny of war stands all the more terribly revealed. Probably no memorial could be more expressive. In June 1915 a young officer named Douglas Gillespie, writing from the front line, proposed a plan for securing general remembrance of war's meaning. To quote him: "Here the Germans are almost on three sides of us, and the dead have been buried just where they fell, behind the trenches. There are graves scattered up and down, some with crosses and names upon them, some nameless and unmarked—as I think my brother's grave must be, for they

have been fighting round about the village where he was killed all
through these last eight months. That doesn't trouble me much,
for πᾶσα γῆ τάφος, but still, these fields are sacred in a sense, and
I wish that when the peace comes, our Government might com-
bine with the French Government to make one long avenue
between the lines from the Vosges to the sea, or if that is too much,
at any rate from La Bassée to Ypres. . . . I would make a fine broad
road in the No Man's Land between the lines, with paths for
pilgrims on foot, and plant trees for shade, and fruit trees, so that
the soil should not be altogether waste. Some of the shattered
farms and houses might be left as evidence, and the regiments
might put up their records beside the trenches which they held all
through the winter. Then I would like to send every man, woman,
and child in Western Europe on pilgrimage along that Via Sacra,
so that they might think and learn what war means from the silent
witnesses on either side. . . . "

This noble-minded young officer was killed on 25 September
1915; his vision of a Via Sacra, which was for a time eagerly
discussed in the public prints, was not to come true. But no one
who has seen the cemeteries which are essentially the theme of the
following pages can doubt that altogether they form a Via Sacra
even more beautiful and more impressive than that of his waking
dream in a dugout towards La Bassée just before an angry dawn.

EDMUND BLUNDEN

THE REPORT

I N T H E S P R I N G O F 1922 King George V made a pilgrimage to
the British War Cemeteries in France and Belgium and, on its
termination, said in a speech delivered in Terlincthun Cemetery,
near Boulogne: "In the course of my pilgrimage, I have many
times asked myself whether there can be more potent advocates of
peace upon earth, through the years to come, than this massed
multitude of silent witnesses to the desolation of war."

These words may be fittingly recalled at the commencement of
an account of the work of the Imperial War Graves Commission;
for they have been a constant inspiration to those engaged in that
work, and have kept ever before their minds the future, as well as
the immediate, purpose of the permanent and visible commemoration of the dead of the Great War.

Twenty years ago, on 21 May 1917, the Royal Charter, under
which the Imperial War Graves Commission are incorporated,
was granted by His Majesty in Council on a recommendation made
by the Imperial War Conference in April of that year. Since then
three Supplemental Charters, recommended by the Imperial
Conference in 1921, 1923 and 1930 respectively, have been
granted; and it is thought that it may interest the Imperial
Conference which is meeting again this year to have before it a
report in general terms on the work accomplished by the Commission, now that, in the light of the experience gained in these
two decades, the course to be pursued in the future is clearly
indicated.

No record of this work would convey the spirit which has per-
vaded it if due acknowledgment were not made at the outset of the

part played by the British Armies in the Field in 1914 in laying the foundations. That it should be made is certainly the desire of men still in the Commission's service, or their immediate successors, who twenty-three years ago realised that the conditions of warfare in which the British Empire was involved demanded an attention to the dead less perfunctory and more systematic than could be paid by the existing army organisation, strained beyond the limits of its means and powers. It was fortunate that in those early days on the Western Front there was an Adjutant-General, Sir Nevil Macready, with breadth of vision and a deep understanding of human sentiment, who immediately lent a sympathetic ear to their proposals. He advised the Commander-in-Chief, Sir John French, to obtain War Office sanction for the creation of a Graves Registration organisation as an integral part of the Army in the Field.*

The Directorate of Graves Registration and Enquiries, created in 1916, soon found that new responsibilities accrued as the scope of the work widened. British soldiers were dying in theatres of war more remote than France and Belgium, and men from all parts of His Majesty's Dominions were rallying to the defence of the Empire. On every field of battle, soldiers of the United Kingdom fell and were buried side by side with their comrades from Canada, Australia, New Zealand, South Africa and Newfoundland, from

* The work had at first been carried out, within the limitation of their powers, by the Joint War Committee of the British Red Cross Society and the Order of St John of Jerusalem. In September 1914, at the suggestion of Lord Kitchener, the Committee sent out a Mobile Unit to search for missing soldiers along the line of the retreat and advance between the Aisne and the Ourcq. During the first battle of Ypres, the Unit was attached to the French I Cavalry Corps, and later, behind Arras, to the French X Corps, and was engaged extensively in carrying French wounded from the battle-front to the hospitals. It was provided at its own request by the Red Cross Society with the means to mark and register British graves in whatever area they might be found. This Mobile Unit with its personnel was taken over and enlarged by the Army in October 1915.

India and from all the British Colonies. The powers of the Director were therefore extended, as a Director-General, to all the theatres of war and he was made directly responsible to the Adjutant-General to the Forces at the War Office, to which post General Macready had been promoted.* One of the Director's first duties was to meet the demand of relatives—more insistent as the numbers of non-professional soldiers forming the New Armies increased—that provision should be made for the care of the graves after the War. It was immediately evident that any permanent body formed for this purpose should reflect the spirit of the free co-operation of the Dominions with the United Kingdom during the War and that its administration after the War should be civilian and above all responsible directly to all the partner Governments of the Empire. As a result, proposals based on these requirements were submitted to and approved by the Imperial War Conference of 1917 and the Imperial War Graves Commission came into being.†

* He was succeeded later as Adjutant-General by Sir George Macdonogh, a no less staunch supporter of the Commission's work both then and since, and still one of the Commission's most active members.

† In January 1916, Dominion representatives had been appointed to a National Committee for the Care of Soldiers' Graves, of which the Prince of Wales was President. In March of the following year, His Royal Highness submitted to the Prime Minister a Memorandum incorporating the proposals of the Director-General of Graves Registration and Enquiries for the formation of a permanent Imperial organisation and asking that the matter might be considered by the Imperial Conference which was to meet that Spring in London under the Chairmanship of Mr Walter Long, Secretary of State for the Colonies. The Memorandum was accompanied by a draft Charter constituting an Imperial War Graves Commission, which should be empowered to care for and maintain the graves of those fallen in the War, to acquire land for the purpose of cemeteries and to erect permanent memorials in the cemeteries and elsewhere. The Memorandum and the Draft Charter (which had been drawn up by the Director-General with the assistance of Captain (later Sir John) Brooke and of the Legal Adviser to the Colonial Office and in consultation with Lord Derby, Lord Milner and other Ministers) were placed first on the Agenda of the Conference. The Charter was examined clause by clause and, with a few amendments, was unanimously approved. On 13 April 1917 a resolution recommending its adoption was moved by Sir

For a year, amid the stress of the closing stages of the war, the Commission deliberated and prepared their plans. Their recommendations and estimates were considered by the Imperial War Conference of 1918, which in June of that year passed the following resolution:*

" The Conference desires to place on record its appreciation of the labours of the Imperial War Graves Commission and is in favour of the cost of the carrying out the decisions of the Commission being borne by the respective Governments in proportion to the numbers of the graves of their dead."

THE EMPIRE'S MILLION DEAD

The immensity of the Empire's losses in the Great War is difficult for the imagination to grasp. It is simple to give statistics, and the following table shows the total number of graves, identified and unidentified, and also the number of those who have been finally recorded as missing and who have been commemorated on Memorials.

Total graves (including 180,861 unidentified)	767,978
Total identified graves	587,117
Total missing commemorated	517,773
Total death casualties	1,104,890

Robert Borden, Prime Minister of Canada, and on 21 May the Royal Charter was granted. H.R.H. the Prince of Wales was the first President of the Commission, Lord Derby the first Chairman and Sir Fabian Ware, who had been Director-General of Graves Registration and Enquiries, the Vice-Chairman. (A full list of Commissioners is given in Appendix A.) For 2½ years after the Armistice the two organisations, the Directorate and the Commission, existed side by side for their several purposes. The higher appointments of the Directorate on 11 November 1918, with a note covering certain subsequent appointments, are given in Appendix C.

* Moved by Sir Robert Borden, Prime Minister of Canada and seconded by Mr W. M. Hughes, Prime Minister of Australia.

THE CROSS OF SACRIFICE

An attempt was made in a broadcast one Armistice Day to give reality to the figures by asking listeners to picture the million dead marching past the Cenotaph:

"Imagine them moving in one long continuous column, four abreast; as the head of that column reaches the Cenotaph the last four men would be at Durham. In Canada that column would stretch across the land from Quebec to Ottawa; in Australia from Melbourne to Canberra; in South Africa from Bloemfontein to Pretoria; in New Zealand from Christchurch to Wellington; in Newfoundland from coast to coast of the Island, and in India from Lahore to Delhi. It would take these million men eighty-four hours, or three and a half days, to march past the Cenotaph in London."

But nothing brings the stern facts home more forcibly than a visit to the cemeteries and memorials. Those who have accompanied visitors to the battlefields in France and Belgium are accustomed to the shock which they experience when, on the confines of the territory for ever made sacred by our men, they are faced with the great northern outpost of the dead at Lijssenthoek, with its 12,000 graves. During the first day of their visit, on their way from cemetery to cemetery, they pass under the Arch of the Menin Gate and find themselves in a vast hall curtained by long files of names, ascending and descending to left and to right, before and behind, the names of 55,000 men who have no known graves. And in a few poignant hours their minds move from bewilderment to reflection under the force of mere numbers which bring a new revelation or perhaps the sting of a forgotten remembrance that should never be absent from their thoughts.

PRINCIPLES AND PLANS

To guide them in dealing with the vast multitude of graves the Commission formulated, and obtained approval for, three general

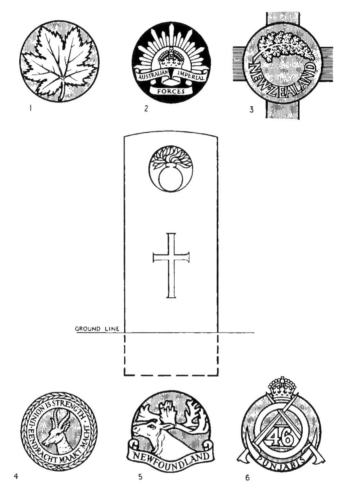

THE HEADSTONE

The headstone stands 2 ft. 8 ins. above ground, is 1 ft. 3 ins. broad and 3 ins. thick, and bears, in addition to the badge and cross or other appropriate religious emblem, the name, rank, unit, date of death and age. At the foot is a personal inscription chosen by the relatives.

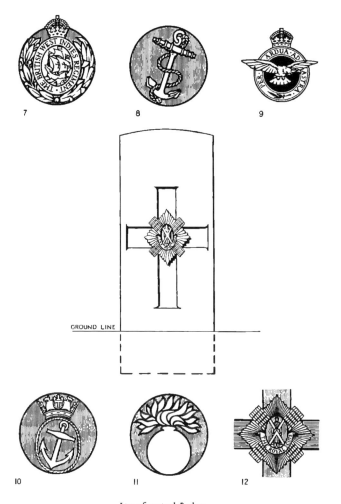

7   8   9

GROUND LINE

10   11   12

List of typical Badges

1. Canada. 2. Australia. 3. New Zealand. 4. South Africa. 5. Newfoundland.
6. India (46th Punjabis). 7. British West Indies. 8. Royal Navy. 9. Royal Air Force.
10. Merchant Navy. 11. Grenadier Guards. 12. The Royal Scots.

principles to control the work of construction: (1) the memorials should be permanent, (2) the headstones should be uniform, and (3) there should be no distinction made on account of military or civil rank. These principles, which were approved by the Imperial Conference of 1918, were further tested, so far as concerned the United Kingdom, by a debate in the House of Commons on 4 May 1920, when the second and third principles were discussed and Mr Winston Churchill lucidly explained the Commission's policy. The matter was left to the free judgment of the House, and a resolution disagreeing with these principles was negatived without a division.

The Commission then proceeded on their labours with the practically unanimous support of public opinion both in the United Kingdom and in the Dominions. The result, as far as the graves are concerned, may be summarised as follows. Some 678,000 headstones have been made and erected—the great majority of them made of British stone and by British labour.* Varieties of stone have had to be used to stand varying climatic conditions, but most of the headstones are of Portland stone. The Commission have constructed in all some 1850 cemeteries and plots, the smallest containing 40 and the largest some 12,000 graves. Nearly 1000 of these cemeteries have been constructed in France and Belgium.†

The general plan of the cemeteries—the two central memorials, the Cross of Sacrifice and the Stone of Remembrance, and the headstones, alike for all, without distinction of rank or station—is well known. The system under which the architects carried out their share of the labours is perhaps less generally familiar.

At their first meeting in November 1917, the Commission were

* The design of the headstone was suggested by a committee of artists which included Mr D. S. MacColl (Keeper of the Wallace Collection), Mr (afterwards Sir) Charles Holmes (Director of the National Gallery) and Mr Macdonald Gill.

† The graves are scattered all over the world; at the end of the book will be found a list of the countries with the numbers of cemeteries and graves in each.

faced with the choice between throwing open a multitude of designs to public competition or themselves selecting one or two architects of outstanding reputation and leaving it to them to agree on the general principles. Tentative efforts made in the latter direction did not prove very successful, and the Commission invited Sir Frederic Kenyon, then Director of the British Museum, to act as their Architectural Adviser. He visited France and Belgium in the winter of 1917–1918, and in the general report which he submitted he proposed that the designing of the cemeteries should be entrusted in the first instance to young architects who had served in the War, but that principal architects of note, each in charge of a definite area, should be appointed to supervise and approve their work.* This simple solution, reviving in some measure the relations between the medieval master architect and his school, overcame most of the difficulties foreseen or hitherto experienced. In retrospect, the chief merit of this system is seen to have been the variety of treatment which resulted from the free play thus given to the interest in individual cemeteries natural to architects who were dealing with the burial places of their comrades in arms.

"KNOWN UNTO GOD"

The Commission were faced with another problem: the commemoration of the many thousands who had no known grave. For, in addition to the erection of headstones over identified graves, and of headstones bearing the inscription "Known unto

---

* The work in France and Belgium was, under this arrangement, entrusted to four principal architects: Sir Edwin Lutyens, Mr (now Sir) Reginald Blomfield, Mr (now Sir) Herbert Baker and Mr Charles Holden. The late Sir Robert Lorimer was the architect responsible for the cemeteries in Egypt, Italy, Greece, Germany and the United Kingdom; Sir John Burnet for those in Gallipoli, Palestine and Syria, and Major Edward Warren for those in Iraq.

God" over unidentified graves, the Commission had to give effect to the desire of relatives (to which moving reference had been made in the House of Commons on the occasion mentioned above) that the Missing Dead should be permanently commemorated, individually and by name, as near as possible to the places where they fell. The "Missing" Memorials were the result. The first of these to be erected, and still to many the best known, was the Menin Gate at Ypres, which records the names of 54,896 officers and men who were killed in the Ypres salient. The history of the origin and development of these memorials is interesting.

In the year 1919 an influential National Battlefields Memorial Committee was appointed by the United Kingdom Government to advise on the erection of Battle Memorials on the Western Front. Representatives of the Dominions served on this Committee.* In its report it indicated the site of the Menin Gate and the neighbourhood of La Ferté-sous-Jouarre as suitable localities for two such memorials. Among its other recommendations was the placing of tablets in some of the cathedrals in the area in which British troops operated.

The United Kingdom Government decided, however, that the large memorials required for the commemoration of the missing would in themselves most suitably record the feats of arms in which those whose names they bore had participated, and it agreed that the Commission should design these memorials to meet the dual requirements so far as the United Kingdom was concerned. The plans of the Dominion Governments for their Battle Memorials were by then well advanced, some being actually in the course of erection. New Zealand, in particular, being able from the records of her more compact forces to commemorate her missing in the cemeteries themselves, proceeded independently from the outset;

* For list of Members see Appendix E.

but all the others decided to join the United Kingdom in recording on the Menin Gate the names of their missing who had fallen in Belgian territory.

In commemorating those who had fallen in France this joint action was not pursued; South Africa alone, having completed her impressive memorial in Delville Wood on which the names of the missing were not recorded, continued to associate herself with the United Kingdom and the names of the missing of both countries appear everywhere side by side. The others decided to commemorate their missing on their own Battle Memorials. Canada, Australia, Newfoundland and India selected as their sites, Vimy, Villers-Bretonneux, Beaumont-Hamel and Neuve-Chapelle respectively. All their memorials have been completed with the exception of the Australian memorial at Villers-Bretonneux; this will be finished in 1938, when the erection on the battlefields of memorials to the Empire's Dead of the Great War will have been completed.*

The memorials to the sailors who died in the Great War, and of whom only a minority had any grave but the sea, may be classed among the "Missing" Memorials.

In 1920, the Admiralty appointed a Naval Memorials Committee to advise the Commission on the most suitable form of monument to the 25,567 ranks and ratings who had lost their lives at sea. This Committee decided on three monuments at the three manning ports, Chatham, Portsmouth and Plymouth, and recommended that they should take the form of a sea-mark or leading-mark near the foreshore, thus combining the memorial with a beacon to

---

* The Commission, being satisfied that when the names were engraved on these memorials they would present an adequate commemoration, decided to make a grant to each of the Governments concerned of a sum calculated on the basis of the cost incurred in commemorating the rest of the missing in France and Belgium. The actual cost of construction was borne by the Governments themselves.

guide ships into their home port. The three monuments, which are similar in design, have been built on the Hoe at Plymouth, on Southsea Common at Portsmouth and on the Great Lines at Chatham.

The Dominions decided that the dead of their naval forces should be commemorated in the following ways. The names of those ranks and ratings of the Royal Canadian Navy who were buried or lost at sea are engraved on two memorials in Canada (at Halifax, Nova Scotia, and Victoria, British Columbia, close to the Atlantic and Pacific naval bases); the Royal Australian Navy and the South African Royal Naval Volunteer Reserve on the Plymouth Memorial; the Newfoundland Royal Naval Reserve at Beaumont-Hamel and in Newfoundland, and the Royal Indian Marine at Bombay. The Chinese seamen of the Royal Navy are commemorated at Hong Kong, and the Indian, Adenese and East African seamen of the Royal Navy with the Royal Indian Marine at Bombay.

On the historic site of Tower Hill, London, a memorial has been erected to the officers and men of the Merchant Navy and Fishing Fleets who lost their lives through enemy action and whose graves are not known. In this service—responsible for carrying by sea the necessities of warfare and those of civil life, for supplying and recruiting the Royal Navy, and for the mine-sweeping which alone made their other tasks practicable—twelve thousand officers and men sank without a trace, and 3300 vessels were destroyed by raiding cruiser or by submarine.

The Commission developed and carried out the suggestion, made by the National Battlefields Memorial Committee, of placing tablets in cathedrals abroad. That the total losses of the British Empire might thus be visibly recorded, a tablet was designed incorporating the arms of the United Kingdom surrounded by those of the Dominions and bearing, for use in France, the following inscription:

TO THE GLORY OF GOD

AND TO THE MEMORY OF

ONE MILLION DEAD

OF THE BRITISH EMPIRE

WHO FELL

IN THE GREAT WAR

1914–1918

AND OF WHOM THE

GREATER PART REST

IN FRANCE

The inscription on the tablets in the cathedrals in France is followed by a translation in French. In Belgium, by agreement with the Belgian ecclesiastical authorities, the translation is in Latin, a convenient alternative to the use of the two languages officially recognised in that country.*

The latest to be erected was unveiled last May by Mr Duff Cooper, the Chairman of the Commission, in Arras Cathedral, the restoration of which had been completed only a few months earlier. A similar tablet placed in the Warrior's Chapel in Westminster Abbey was unveiled by the Prince of Wales, in 1926, when the occasion of the meeting of the Imperial Conference was used for assembling, on Mr Baldwin's invitation, the Prime Ministers and

* These tablets have been erected in each of the following cathedrals or churches: in France, Notre Dame (Paris), Amiens, Arras, Bayeux, Beauvais, Bethune, Boulogne-sur-Mer, Cambrai, Laon, Le Mans, Lille, Marseilles, Meaux, Nancy, Nantes, Noyon, Orleans, Reims, Rouen, St Omer, St Quentin, Senlis, Soissons; in Belgium, Brussels, Antwerp, Malines, Mons and Ypres.

representatives of all the partner Governments for a brief religious
service. The following prayer was used:

"O God, the creator and preserver of all mankind, Ruler of the world,
who has entrusted to the Governments of our Commonwealth the care
of many peoples in distant lands: grant we beseech Thee that the
members of our wide-spread Empire may ever be bound together in
mutual love and unity under our Sovereign Lord the King. Give to
those who have the responsibility of Government and administration
wisdom, patience and courage, and grant we humbly pray Thee that
at this time the guidance of Thy Holy Spirit may be with them in their
deliberations so that all that is now said and done shall be for the good
of our nations, the welfare of mankind and the spread of Thy Kingdom
throughout the world, through Jesus Christ our Lord."

The Commission regretted that the arrangements which they
had made with the Dean and Chapter for the repetition of this
service on the opening of the Imperial Conference in 1930 were
cancelled.

These cathedral tablets are the first and only memorials to
express in sculptured form the union of the partner nations in the
British Commonwealth under one Crown. They have been called
the coping-stone of the Commission's work.

THE REGISTER OF NAMES

To provide a record in accordance with the directions of the
Charter, possibly even more permanent than that which has been
described, a series of printed Registers—one for every cemetery or
memorial—has been published. Each Register contains an alpha-
betical list of the dead, with such brief biographical details as
could be obtained by direct communication with the relatives; a
statement of the circumstances in which the cemetery or the

THE STONE OF REMEMBRANCE

ETAPLES MILITARY CEMETERY, FRANCE

BAC-DU-SUD BRITISH CEMETERY, FRANCE

WAILLY ORCHARD CEMETERY, FRANCE

YPRES RESERVOIR CEMETERY, BELGIUM

BERKS CEMETERY EXTENSION AND
PLOEGSTEERT MEMORIAL, BELGIUM

WHITE HOUSE CEMETERY, ST JEAN, BELGIUM

COLOGNE SOUTHERN CEMETERY, GERMANY

CAVALETTO BRITISH CEMETERY, ITALY

LAHANA MILITARY CEMETERY, GREECE

memorial was made; and, where necessary, a map of the surrounding country and a detailed plan. Nearly a thousand Register parts, each containing about a thousand names, have been completed; of the few yet to be published, the majority must await the gradual completion of the last few cemeteries.

In these, bodies found on the battlefields are still being buried. Even before hostilities had ceased a careful search was made for scattered graves. It was continued in a more systematic form after the Armistice, the front being divided for the purpose into areas, each under a party of twelve men and a senior N.C.O. Between the Armistice and September 1921, 204,650 bodies were taken from the battlefields and reburied in cemeteries set aside to receive them. Since that date, no further general search has been undertaken, but 38,000 more bodies have been found by farmers, metal-searchers and others, and they are still coming to light at the rate of twenty to thirty a week. Arrangements have been made for proper notification to the Commission. Each body is reburied with due reverence in the nearest of those cemeteries in which land is specially reserved for the purpose and the grave marked with a headstone. About 20 per cent have been identified, and it is still possible to identify from 10 to 15 per cent of the bodies discovered.

INTERNATIONAL RELATIONS

Much might be written on the Commission's relations with foreign Governments. In the lands both of former allies and of former enemies lie the graves of men from all parts of the British Empire, a permanent link between our own and other peoples. In all these lands the Commission have been accorded formal recognition as the properly constituted authority charged with the care of

British military cemeteries and graves.* On the cessation of hostilities, homage to the dead who had fallen in a common effort was a natural outcome and continuation of the friendships formed in a long war, but the Commission at that date were not conscious of any mission to extend this common commemoration beyond the formidable barriers left by the War.

Once again, King George V pointed the way. In the speech of May 1922, from which a quotation has already been given, the King expressed the hope that "the existence of these visible memorials will, eventually, serve to draw all peoples together in sanity and self-control, even as it has already set the relations between our Empire and our allies on the deep-rooted bases of a common heroism and a common agony".

Nor in this connection should the influence be forgotten of the late Monseigneur Julien, Bishop of Arras, with whom the Commission's work frequently brought them into contact. One of the leaders of the French people in the worthy commemoration of their own dead, he never ceased to remind them that "in the sight of God the dead of Germany were the equals of the dead of France". Following no expressed policy, but guided rather by the feeling that the dead should be allowed to speak for themselves, the Commission did little more at first than refrain from placing any obstacles in the way of this spiritual intercourse; nothing was allowed to be said in any inscription which would tend to perpetuate international ill-will, and enemy graves in British military cemeteries were planted and tended with the same care as those of our own soldiers.

As the years have gone by, the old hatreds, never so intense in the trenches as behind the lines, have been merged in a common

---

* In Turkey the responsibilities of the Commission were, by an exchange of letters at the Montreux Conference in 1936, given due recognition for the future. Formal recognition of the Commission as elsewhere has not yet been accorded.

pity and a common recognition of heroism, until at last the Commission have been able to unite France, Germany and the British
Commonwealth in an organised movement of common remembrance of the dead of the Great War.

The history of the international organisations established by the
Commission may be briefly described. In the first year of the War,
as casualties grew heavy, it became necessary to establish contact
with the French civil authorities to arrange for the acquisition of
the land required for burials. The French Government decided that
the necessary provision should be a charge on the French people.
Other allied countries showed equal generosity, and former
enemy countries after the War satisfied our desire to obtain
permanent resting places for our dead.*

Perpetuity of sepulture was thus assured; but further arrangements had to be made for permanent maintenance and to give
effect to the desire of the relatives that the guardians of the graves
should be men of one race with the dead. This desire could only
be achieved by international agreements, under which foreign

* Early in 1915, it was realised that the practice of burying British soldiers in local
civil cemeteries in France could not be indefinitely continued and it became necessary
to acquire new land for cemetery purposes.
On the instructions of Sir Nevil Macready the question was taken up in Paris by the
Officer Commanding the Graves Registration organisation, who, as the representative
of the Adjutant-General, was authorised to be the "sole intermediary between the
British Army in the Field and the French military and civil authorities in all matters
relating to graves". Since there were obvious objections in France to the acquisition of
land in the name of foreign Governments, the problem presented some difficulty; but
owing to the generosity of the French Government a solution was found in the French
law which was approved by both Chambers on 29 December 1915. This law provided
for the acquisition by, and at the expense of, the French State of all lands required
outside existing cemeteries as the burial places of French and allied soldiers dying in the
War. A later French Decree of 25 September 1920 provided perpetual sepulture, at the
expense of the State, for French and allied soldiers resting in the communal burial
grounds.
The law of December 1915 became the model which has in general been followed

countries would transfer to the Commission powers and privileges which of right belonged to themselves.

As early as the spring of 1916, the British Government had intimated to the French Government that when the War was over it would wish to assume entire responsibility for the upkeep of the British cemeteries on French soil.

In May of that year, a Joint Anglo-French Committee was appointed at British General Headquarters to discuss at regular meetings certain matters regarding the cemeteries in which it was necessary and useful at the time, or in view of future contingencies, to secure the co-operation of the French. The Anglo-French-Belgian Agreement of August 1917, under which the Belgian Government agreed to acquire, at its own cost, such lands as were needed for our cemeteries, also provided that these cemeteries

by the other late allied countries. In each case, the State has acquired the site and has handed over the perpetual enjoyment ("jouissance") to the Commission.

The principal laws, agreements or assurances relating to acquisition in different countries are as follows:

France. Laws of 29 December 1915 and 25 September 1920.

Belgium. Anglo-Franco-Belgian Agreement of 9 August 1917.

Italy. Decree of 23 June 1918.

Greece. Anglo-Greek Agreement of 7/20 November 1918 followed by Expropriation Decrees of 23 July/5 August 1921 and 10/23 November 1921.

Palestine. Gift by the Government of Palestine in conjunction with the Municipalities concerned.

Iraq. Gift by the Government of Iraq or acquisition by the Commission.

Egypt. Deed of Gift dated 9 May 1921.

Germany. Treaty of Versailles. Federal Law of 29 December 1922.

Turkey. Treaty of Lausanne. At the Montreux Conference in July 1936, an undertaking was given by the Turkish Government to "continue to maintain the same facilities as in the past in regard to the upkeep and supervision of, and to visits to, the cemeteries, and in regard to the application of Article 124 of the Treaty of Lausanne."

Land for the Memorials to the Missing has in many cases been provided free of cost by the generosity of the State or of Municipalities; in others it has been acquired by the Commission.

should be handed over to the British Government for construction and maintenance in perpetuity.

In June 1918, however, the French Government felt that the time had come to organise the maintenance of the hundreds of thousands of war graves on French soil, and the Vice-Chairman of the Commission was instructed and empowered by Lord Milner, Secretary of State for War and Chairman of the Commission, to discuss the subject personally with M. Clemenceau, Prime Minister of France. The interview with M. Clemenceau took place in July, and, as a result, a Constituent Committee was set up which was a direct offspring of the Joint Anglo-French Committee at General Headquarters and which, in turn, led to the Anglo-French Mixed Committee, created under the Anglo-French Agreement signed in Paris on 26 November 1918.

This Agreement recognised the right of the Commission to act as the properly constituted authority (the "association regulière-ment constituée" of the French Law of 29 December 1915), charged with the care of all British military cemeteries and graves; and under it the French Government undertook to afford the Commission the necessary facilities for carrying out constructional and maintenance work. At the same time, it established in the "Mixed Committee" an "Agency" which possesses the special capacity of representing the Commission in their day-to-day relations with the French civil and military authorities.

The Anglo-French Mixed Committee is composed of honorary and official members, the British and Dominion representation and the French representation being equal. All the members are appointed by the Commission although, so far as the French members are concerned, the appointments are made on the re-commendation of the French Government.

The Committee first met on 6 May 1919 and has since met

thirteen times under the Chairmanship of General de Castelnau, to whose deep personal sympathy and wise guidance the happy development of this new venture in international administration is largely due. And one other French name must be mentioned—that of Intendant Général Vincensini, K.B.E., head of the French War Graves Service in the Ministère des Pensions and, as such, a member of the Committee since 1925. General Vincensini's British colleagues have learnt to trust his judgment, to value his friendship and to rely on his loyalty; and the spirit of frank and sympathetic collaboration in which the two services work has been one of the most powerful influences in the movement of common remembrance to which reference has already been made.

The Anglo-French Agreement of November 1918 provided the model for a series of other international Agreements under which "Mixed Committees"* on similar lines have been established. The Anglo-Belgian Agreement was signed on 13 June 1919, the Anglo-Greek on 27 August/9 September 1921, the Anglo-Italian on 11 May 1922 and the Anglo-German-French on 20 December 1935; and the Committees have met from time to time as occasion required.

The Anglo-German-French Agreement is the first of its kind to be made with an ex-enemy country. It is unique in that the Mixed Committee which it has created functions also reciprocally as the representative of the German Government in all matters relating to German war graves in British territory and in British cemeteries in France. The Committee first met in London on 8 June 1936, under the Chairmanship of Viscount Trenchard.

---

* Among the foreign representatives on these committees have been: M. Ernest Lavisse and M. Paul Painlevé (France); M. Paul Hymans (Belgium); Marshal Diaz (Italy); Professor André Andreades (Greece); and Herr von Hoesch and Generaloberst von Seeckt (Germany). The original membership of the Anglo-German-French Committee—built up on the model of the four earlier Committees—is set out in Appendix D.

In a speech welcoming his German and French colleagues, Lord Trenchard said: "I believe that the formation of this Committee may prove to be, in its way, a turning-point in human affairs. We have already, each in the manner which seemed to us most fitting, honoured our fallen comrades. May it not be that in this wider remembrance of them all, and in common and constant recalling of their heroism and their sacrifice, we may be permitted to hear their voice speaking for themselves and guiding our feet into the way of peace?"

For the conclusion of these Agreements lengthy negotiations with foreign Governments have often been necessary. And in all the Agreements negotiated since the War the Commission had, even before the Statute of Westminster indicated the necessity, carried out in accordance with their constitution the duty of obtaining the approval of each of the other participating Governments of the British Commonwealth as well as that of the United Kingdom. Under their Charter the concurrence of the Foreign Office in particular is required for entering into relations with a foreign Government; to that Office and to the offices in the Dominions concerned with external affairs and to the British Ambassadors, as well as to Dominion Ministers, in the foreign countries concerned, the Commission have owed largely the success which has attended their efforts. The names of eight—Lord Derby, Sir Francis Villiers, Lord Rennell, Lord Tyrrell, Dr Philippe Roy (of Canada), Sir Francis Humphrys, Sir Eric Phipps and Dr S. F. N. Gie (of South Africa)—stand out as active participators and friendly sympathisers in the steps which the Commission have taken to achieve this object.

The Commission maintain Agencies, in the form of Committees, in Iraq and Palestine. As long as Iraq remained a mandated territory, a Committee with wider powers than those of the Western

Mixed Committees operated in that country. This Committee was known as the Iraq War Graves Committee and held its first meeting in October 1922. In 1930, with the recognition of Iraq as an independent state, it became necessary to bring the Committee into closer conformity as to powers with those established in European countries. This was carried out under the Anglo-Iraqi War Graves Agreement of 15 March 1935. The constitution of this Committee, however, differs from that of the others in that its members are appointed on the sole nomination of the British Ambassador in Baghdad (who is *ex officio* Chairman) and are at present exclusively British.

The Anglo-Palestine War Cemeteries Executive Committee, which grew out of an informal Committee appointed by the High Commissioner in 1920, was formally constituted as an Agency of the Commission on 13 October 1926. This Committee still retains its original wide scope and powers.

In Egypt, an Anglo-Egyptian War Cemeteries Executive Committee, which developed from an earlier organisation, was established as an Agency of the Commission on 4 February 1921. The Commission's relations with Egypt are, however, under revision in view of the changed status of the country since the general Anglo-Egyptian Treaty of 1936.

In certain of the Dominions and Colonies, the Commission have also found that the most convenient method of discharging their responsibility has been to appoint an Agent or Agency to whom certain of their powers are delegated by legal instrument.

In Canada, the Minister of National Defence acts as the Agency, the executive work being carried out from an office in Ottawa by the Secretary-General* and a small staff employed by the Commission. In South Africa, the Chairman of the Agency is the

* Colonel H. C. Osborne, C.M.G., C.B.E.

CANTERBURY CEMETERY, ANZAC, GALLIPOLI

JERUSALEM WAR CEMETERY

KUT WAR CEMETERY, IRAQ

MENIN GATE, YPRES, 1914

MENIN GATE, YPRES, 1918

MENIN GATE MEMORIAL, YPRES

CANADIAN NATIONAL MEMORIAL, VIMY, FRANCE
(BUILT BY THE CANADIAN BATTLEFIELDS MEMORIALS
COMMISSION)

AUSTRALIAN NATIONAL MEMORIAL, VILLERS-BRETONNEUX,
FRANCE (NOW UNDER CONSTRUCTION)

NEW ZEALAND MEMORIAL IN BUTTES NEW BRITISH CEMETERY,
POLYGON WOOD, BELGIUM

Secretary for Public Works of the Government of the Union, and the Secretary,* who is an official of the Commission, has headquarters at Pretoria. In India, H.E. the Governor-General in Council has acted as the Commission's Agent and administered the funds granted by the Commission for the upkeep of graves in that country. This arrangement, however, is now subject to review following the recent constitutional changes under the Government of India Act (1935). In both Malta and Gibraltar, the Governor and Commander-in-Chief is the Chairman of the Agency, the Secretary in each case being an officer of the military garrison.

In East Africa, the Governments of Kenya, Tanganyika and Nyasaland have undertaken the maintenance of war graves in their respective territories free of charge to the Commission. The Ceylon and Zanzibar Governments also maintain at their own cost all war graves under their control.

The Governments of Australia and New Zealand have accepted full responsibility for the construction and maintenance at their own cost of war graves in their respective territories, and they have treated as such the graves of all soldiers who died as a result of war service without regard to the legal termination of the War on 31 August 1921.

In the Irish Free State the graves are marked with the Commission's form of headstone, the Government itself having undertaken the work at its own cost. A representative of the Commission was placed at its disposal to advise and assist it.

It is sometimes surprising to discover how little is generally known of the many war graves in the United Kingdom and Northern Ireland—90,000 of them in 10,000 cemeteries and churchyards. There are 385 cemeteries in which there is a sufficient number to have justified the erection of a Cross of

* Captain J. G. Marais.

Sacrifice. In many, notably in Brookwood Cemetery, Surrey, lie soldiers from the Dominions overseas, and the Women's Institutes and Women's Section of the British Legion take special interest in these graves by arrangement with the Commission. Sometimes they are in direct correspondence with the relatives who, there is reason to know, take comfort in the thought that British women are watching over graves which are dear to them.

British war graves are to be found in numerous other countries, e.g. the Scandinavian and Baltic countries, Poland, Holland, Persia, Syria, etc., where, in the absence of formal Agencies, the Commission's duties are mainly discharged through the help and good offices of the diplomatic representatives and consular officials.

FINANCE

The proportions of the financial contributions referred to in the resolution of the Imperial Conference of 1918 (quoted on p. 22) were based on figures provisionally agreed for identified graves. In 1930, when, for practical purposes, stability of statistical records had been arrived at, final figures were prepared by the Commission's Director of Records and were accepted by all the Governments. They are as follows:

Government	Identified graves	Percentage
United Kingdom ...	454,574	81·53
Canada	43,391	7·78
Australia	35,408	6·35
New Zealand	10,117	1·81
South Africa	6,340	1·14
India	5,665	1·02
British West Indies ...	1,262	0·23
Newfoundland ...	763	0·14
	557,520	100·00

In addition, there are 180,861 unidentified graves.

The estimate placed before the Conference contemplated an expenditure on constructional work of £10 a grave and £5 on the commemoration of each soldier with no known grave. If these figures are applied to the total number of graves permanently marked by the Commission (738,000) and Missing Dead (518,000) there results a total estimate of approximately £10,000,000. That was the expenditure contemplated. But the total expenditure on construction, allowing for the very small amount yet to be done, amounts to £8,150,000, and thus shows an expenditure of £1,850,000 less than the estimate. This result is due to the strict control exercised by the Finance Committee which was established

in December 1918. A brief statement as to its position and influence in the counsels of the Commission may rightly precede an
account of the Commission's expenditure and sources of revenue.

The Finance Committee was given, at the outset, a special
place in the organisation of the Commission. While its powers of
control were made as effective as those of any corresponding
Finance Committee, wider functions than were usual were
allotted to it. These were indicated by the dual office filled by the
official who was appointed its Secretary; not only was he the
Financial Adviser on the Commission's staff, he was also its
Controller of Administration. In the latter role he was engaged in
the direction of work of a progressively constructional character,
calling both for organisation and for rapid provision of the
financial means of execution. He was thus constantly under an
influence running strongly counter to the natural tendency of a
Secretary to a Finance Committee which is to direct the thoughts
of his Committee primarily to critical and repressive activities.

Starting with this wider outlook, the Finance Committee found
itself before long occupying the key position in the development,
and sometimes in the defence, of an administration based on the
principle of free Imperial co-operation. For it soon became
evident that the equality of political status (to which the War had
given final sanction) of the participating Governments, and their
common contributions to the requisite funds, implied free co-
operation in the control of the Commission's finances. In June
1919, the United Kingdom Government, whose contribution on
the agreed basis represented 81 per cent of the total, was, on
the suggestion of Sir George Perley, then High Commissioner for
Canada, approached through the Chancellor of the Exchequer
by representatives of the other Governments and the Vice-Chairman. The Chancellor of the Exchequer undertook that the United

Kingdom proportion of the estimated annual expenditure should be provided in the form of a grant-in-aid, thus rendering expenditure independent of United Kingdom Treasury control.

The financial autonomy thus secured to the Commission was in principle unconditional. But, at the request of the Commission, the Chancellor of the Exchequer agreed that a representative of the United Kingdom Treasury should attend the meetings of the Commission's Finance Committee with a view to affording advice and assistance on financial and administrative questions. The practice thus initiated has continued ever since, and has proved of great benefit to the Commission. The fact that the premier Treasury in the Commonwealth has access in this manner to all details of the Commission's current expenditure and financial policy has undoubtedly added to the general confidence in the Commission's financial administration. The Finance Committee has thus acquired, as has been observed, a special, and indeed a unique place, in the first Imperial organisation of this kind. The manner in which it has exercised its powers of control has demonstrated its value as an instrument of Imperial co-operation and has fully justified the hopes of those who were responsible for initiating its organisation.*

* The first members of the Finance Committee were Sir Alfred Mond, Bart., M.P., the Rt Hon. W. P. Schreiner, K.C., Harry Gosling, Esq., M.P., Major-General Sir Fabian Ware (Chairman) and Lieut.-Colonel C. D. Branch, M.C. (Secretary). It will be seen from the following list of members that the Commission have been fortunate in obtaining the services on this Committee of men of outstanding financial and administrative experience at home and in the Dominions. The number of years for which each served is shown in brackets and those still serving are marked with asterisks: The Rt Hon. Andrew Fisher (1); Sir William Garstin (6); Mr Harry Gosling (13); Sir Alfred Mond (2); *Sir Fabian Ware (18); *Sir Edgar Bowring (4); the Hon. Sir James Allen (7); Sir Robert Hudson (8); *Admiral Sir Morgan Singer (15); Sir Henry Maddocks, K.C. (10); *Lieut.-General Sir George Macdonogh (12); the Rt Hon. Sir Joseph Cook (2); Major-General Sir Granville Ryrie (5); *Mr J. J. Lawson, M.P. (5); *Mr W. P. Spens, K.C., M.P. (5); the Hon. G. H. Ferguson (3); *the Rt Hon. S. M. Bruce (4).

The foregoing paragraphs show that the Commission are directly responsible to each and all of the participating Governments represented for the proper administration of the funds granted by those Governments. In theory the Commission's Chief Accounting Officer (the Vice-Chairman) can be summoned before the Public Accounts Committee of any of the Dominion Parliaments for examination. In practice the Dominions have been satisfied to accept examination by the Public Accounts Committee of the United Kingdom House of Commons before which the Vice-Chairman appears each year.

THE ENDOWMENT FUND

The most far-reaching and important development from the point of view of finance has been the establishment of an Endowment Fund to provide income for the permanent maintenance of the graves, cemeteries and memorials. It was felt by all the participating Governments that the relatives had a right to this recognised form of provision against future contingencies in return for their abandonment, in the common interest, of the claim made by many of them to care for their graves personally.

In 1924 an estimate of the cost of permanent maintenance was prepared amounting to £225,000 a year, this figure being reduced after discussion to £216,000 a year. It was calculated that if a fund were established within a comparatively short time this income could be provided by a capital of five million pounds. The participating Governments were accordingly asked to agree to the establishment of such a fund by means of contributions over a period of six and a half years, by which time it was estimated that constructional work would be complete. It was suggested that the desired result should be achieved by the stabilisation of the contributions from the Governments at the figure for the estimates of the year 1925 over a period of six and a half years. It was anticipated that the remaining constructional work, the maintenance during the transitional period and the accumulation of the capital fund could be met out of these unified contributions, the unspent portion of the annual contributions being allowed to accumulate at interest until the end of the period. All the participating Governments with the exception of the United Kingdom agreed to this proposal and completed their contributions within the specified period. The United Kingdom Government decided however that, their proportion being over $81\frac{1}{2}$ per cent of the whole, their share should be contributed over a period of thirteen and a half years.

Since part of the proposal involved the accumulation of interest, and the Head Office of the Commission was within the United Kingdom jurisdiction, an Act of the United Kingdom Parliament was required to permit of the Endowment Fund being established with the necessary powers. The Imperial War Graves Endowment Bill became law on 30 June 1926. To administer the Fund three Trustees were appointed under Trust Deed, the first three being Sir Herbert Lawrence, Sir Edward Peacock and Sir Fabian Ware; Sir Herbert Ellissen accepted the Secretaryship. In view of the permanent nature of the Fund, the "Imperial War Graves Endowment Fund Trustees" are constituted under that Act an incorporated body with perpetual succession, thus avoiding the inconveniences usually arising when new trustees are appointed.

The Dominion proportion of the Endowment Fund was completed in 1931, well within the estimate prepared in 1924. The Commission's estimates of income and expenditure have, however, been affected by three main factors. The first has been the addition of nearly 40,000 graves discovered on the battlefields or reported to the Commission since 1924. This represents an additional annual charge of certainly not less than £10,000 a year. A second factor of perhaps a more temporary nature has been the alteration in the value of sterling in terms of foreign exchanges which took place in 1931. Until the recent devaluation of the French and Belgian francs the additional cost of foreign exchange has been on an average £50,000 a year since 1931. This additional cost of foreign exchange has been provided as far as possible out of economies effected by the Commission, but the greater part of it has had to be provided by additional Votes by the participating Governments. The third factor has been the alteration in money rates since the conversion of War Loan in the United Kingdom. As a result the Commission's Trustees have latterly been unable to invest the contributions and accumulations of interest of the United Kingdom proportion of the Fund at the favourable rates originally anticipated. Had the United Kingdom Government been prepared to complete their contributions to the Endowment Fund within the period of six and a half years originally suggested, this difficulty would not have occurred. The result so far as it can be foreseen at present is that, while the rate of interest earned on the Dominion portion of the Fund is now $4\frac{3}{4}$ per cent and will so remain until 1940, which is the earliest date on which conversion of any of the Dominions securities concerned can be effected, the rate on the United Kingdom proportion of the Fund already accumulated is under 4 per cent, and the total income may therefore fall short of the minimum total of £216,000 per annum estimated in 1924.

It is too early yet to form any definite conclusions for the future; meanwhile the Finance Committee is introducing all possible economies which may help to meet a deficit should that ultimately have to be faced. It cannot lose sight of the fact, however, that by far the heaviest expenditure is on the wages of the gardener-caretaker staff and that there alone could substantial savings be made, though only at the cost of a lower standard of maintenance.

MAINTENANCE STAFF

The principle of Imperial co-operation on which the Commission were founded is reflected in the composition of the staff, the Dominion personnel representing roughly the proportion of their Governments' contributions to the funds. For example, after considerable thought an understanding was reached that the Commission's chief official in France should be a Canadian, while in the Eastern District (covering Egypt, Palestine, Iraq, Macedonia and Gallipoli) he should be an Australian or a New Zealander.* While it is impossible to apply this principle in full to the lowest paid appointments, there is a number of Dominion personnel among the gardener-caretakers in France and Belgium.

The staff of the Commission serve the Crown, but being responsible to and paid by all the Governments of the Empire they do not belong to, and they cannot enjoy the privileges of, the Civil Service of the United Kingdom or of any one of the participating Governments. Nor is there yet any Commonwealth Civil Service to which they could be attached as servants of the Crown in the full technical sense of the term. The conditions of service and rates of pay of the clerical staff, which numbers 106 in all parts of the world, have been fixed as far as possible to conform with those of the United Kingdom Civil Service. There are, however, as many as 548 members of the wages staff, all but a few of them being gardener-caretakers working in France and Belgium.

The welfare of these men and their families is the constant concern of the Commission. The fact that they live abroad, where they are outside the ordinary scope of the National Health and

* This understanding has been carried out. The present, as the former, holder of this position in France is a Canadian; an Australian was appointed to the similar position in the Eastern District and on his recent retirement was replaced by a New Zealander. (The historic Anzac area of Gallipoli falls within this district.)

Contributory Pensions Acts of the United Kingdom, has presented, and continues to present, many special problems. In 1926 and succeeding years, the large staff required during the period of construction was gradually reduced and the work was reorganised on a basis of Permanent Maintenance. With the agreement of the participating Governments, certain provisions for welfare and children's education were made; but as some doubt existed as to whether these provisions were covered by the Commission's Charter, it was decided that the Imperial Conference, which was meeting in London in October 1930, should be asked to approve an application to the Crown for a Supplemental Charter endowing the Commission with the necessary powers in this direction. The Conference gave its approval and a Supplemental Charter was granted on 12 February 1931.

Among the most important of the welfare measures which were validated by this Supplemental Charter were the introduction, in 1926, of a Superannuation Scheme for all members of the Permanent Maintenance staff, and the extension, in 1930, of medical provision for the families of the staff living in France and Belgium, together with the appointment of a resident medical officer and a trained nurse. In May 1927 a Staff Committee, consisting of Commissioners, had been formed to consider and report on all questions concerning the appointment, conditions of service, superannuation, promotion, etc. of the staff. It has proved a valuable institution, empowered as it is to hear appeals from the staff. It meets as required, and on occasion two or more of its members visit France and Belgium to investigate in person local conditions.

An Education Committee was set up in 1930 to discuss and advise on questions affecting the education of the children of the staff in France and Belgium. This Committee has the active support of the Board of Education and of the Scottish Education Department and meets three or four times a year. The provision of an English education for children living in and around Ypres is a comparatively simple matter, thanks to the existence there of the Eton Memorial School, which was founded on a voluntary basis soon after the War. This school is attended by children of the Commission's staff living in the neighbourhood and receives an annual grant from the Commission. On the other hand, the education of the children living in outlying parts of Belgium and in France, where the families are scattered over a wide area, presents considerable difficulty. A school which the Commission opened in Arras in 1930 had to be closed through lack of support; but a scheme is now successfully in operation whereby maintenance grants are awarded annually to parents to assist them in sending their children to England to be educated. These grants are designed to cover the period of elementary school education in senior schools, that is to say—under the present Law—between the ages of eleven and fourteen. For the benefit of those children who are unable to attend the Eton Memorial School or to come to England to be educated, the Commission conduct free correspondence courses in English subjects in co-operation with the Parents' National Educational Union.

In making appointments to the staff, preference has always been given to ex-Service men of the Great War, but in the last two years, owing to their advancing age, it has been difficult to obtain suitable applicants. Hitherto vacancies have occurred almost entirely amongst the gardeners, and experiments are being made by the training of sons of present employees as pupil gardeners and by the appointment of post-war ex-Army men who have been trained as gardeners at the Army Vocational Training Centre at Chiseldon.

The general high standard of horticultural maintenance of the cemeteries abroad is well known, and is in the main due to the knowledge, experience and constant devotion of the gardening staff, supported and directed, from the first days when the cemeteries were planted, by the advice of Captain (now Sir Arthur) Hill, who since 1922 has been the Director of the Royal Botanic Gardens at Kew. It is only possible to obtain this high standard by attracting men of the right type by means of good wages and tolerable conditions of service. If substantial economies should prove essential, they would have to be made, as has been indicated, at the expense of this branch of the service, either by a reduction in the number employed or by the use of local labour in place of British labour. It is certain that the present standard could not be maintained under either of these alternatives, and there is no doubt that the desire of the public to-day, and in particular of the relatives, is that the graves in France and Belgium should be looked after by gardener-caretakers of their own race.

BUILDING AND CONSTRUCTION

Of the extent of the building operations and works (in the material and technical sense) which the Commission have carried out it is difficult to convey an impression in words. Shortly before his death Rudyard Kipling, looking back on that which had been done since he had joined the Commission as one of their foundation members, remarked, in a characteristic aside, "The biggest single bit of work since any of the Pharaohs—and they only worked in their own country."

To give mere figures, in France and Belgium alone there are 970 architecturally constructed cemeteries surrounded by 50 miles of walling in brick or stone, with nearly 1000 Crosses of Sacrifice and 560 Stones of Remembrance, and many chapels, record buildings and shelters; there are some 600,000 headstones resting on nearly 250 miles of concrete beam foundations. There are also eighteen larger memorials to those who have no known grave, the largest being that to the "Missing of the Somme", on which 73,367 names are engraved.

For that which meets the eye, as one travels from land to land on a pilgrimage to the holy places which the Empire's dead have left to us, the architects and the gardeners must be given the credit. For that which is not seen—foundations and material construction on which the durability of everything depends—the Commission's Directors of Works and Consulting Engineers have been responsible. It is only necessary to mention the first of these consulting engineers, Sir Maurice Fitzmaurice, the President of the Institution of Civil Engineers, to show that here again the best advice available was placed freely at the Commission's disposal. The Commission were also fortunate in having as one of their first and most active members Sir William Garstin, whose name appears side by side with that of Sir Maurice Fitzmaurice on the Assouan Dam on the Nile, one of the greatest engineering feats of modern times.

To such men as these, and to others who were leaders in special branches of scientific experience and research bearing upon construction, the Commission were able to turn in all their difficulties, and these were many: in the matter of foundations alone there were few known to engineers which the Commission's Directors of Works did not encounter. They had to build in the water-logged land around Ypres where, for defence during the War, allies and enemies alike had been forced to construct block-houses above the surface instead of the customary dug-outs underground; on the edge of the moat whose waters lapped the site of the Menin Gate; above the honeycomb of underground workings beneath Tower Hill where the Merchant Navy Memorial now rises; on Southsea Common, with the water a few feet below the surface; amidst the Alpine conditions of the Asiago Plateau in Italy; in the sands of

Egypt, Syria and Iraq; on the river front at Basra at the north end of the Persian Gulf. And on the battlefields of France, Belgium, Gallipoli and Macedonia they were always haunted by one uncertainty of a kind that builders had rarely had to face before; anywhere deep below the surface of a site, however carefully studied beforehand, might lie hidden cavernous dug-outs to be disclosed only as the work progressed.

Added to these difficulties was one about which more will be said later—the diversity of climatic and other conditions demanding the use of special qualities of stone and materials. In the more distant lands there were few, if any, records to show what were the adverse forces of nature to be met and what were the means by which they had been countered in the past.

Generally speaking, it may be said that all these difficulties have been surmounted and that sufficient time has now elapsed since the many buildings were completed to test their construction and prove that it was sound. Even in the Near East the Commission have passed out of the long and trying experimental stage necessitated by the failure of carefully selected qualities of stone to resist the action of the sun above and the salt beneath—two hostile forces which, in the words of the Director of Works, made no discrimination in favour of the Commission's work; but after years of study of their devastating influence he is able to report that they require only to be studied and understood to enable one to escape their ill effects. With the help of some of the foremost chemists and scientists, he has succeeded in doing so. In one or two places, however, such as Amara in Iraq, which is a veritable salt pan, headstones on individual graves have had to be replaced by simple numbered pegs, the names being inscribed on slate panels affixed to a screen wall, and insulated against the attacks of the salt.

PRESERVATION OF HEADSTONES

Apart from the exceptional difficulties, some of which have been mentioned, the duty of structural maintenance is normal in its procedure and in the organisation required. But in the maintenance of the headstones themselves experience has led to a more satisfactory result than was originally foreseen, a result which is doing much to allay the anxiety of relatives, who expressed the fear that the headstones lacked the quality of permanence, and were disturbed by the formula that they would be allowed "to grow old gracefully". Experiments pursued over a sufficiently long period have furnished data which point to a durability far greater than was at first anticipated. By the use of preservatives, by thorough cleansing with pure water and rubbing with sandstone, by re-cutting the lettering where it is found necessary to do so, and by replacement in the few cases where it is essential, practical permanency is now assured. A system has been initiated, and is working well, by which all the headstones will have been so treated by the end of the year 1946, and from that time onwards there should be no difficulty in maintaining a twelve-year cycle for the purpose. While for part of this treatment expert labour is required and provided, the periodical washing of the headstones is entrusted to the gardener-caretakers.

GRAVES OF OTHER WARS

By the original Charter the responsibility of the Commission is strictly limited to the commemoration of those who died in the Great War from wounds inflicted, accident occurring or disease contracted while on active service, but they have been invited by the Government of the United Kingdom and other Governments to take over the maintenance of cemeteries resulting from other wars, particularly the Peninsular and Crimean Wars. To this end a Supplemental Charter was granted on the recommendation of the Imperial Conference in 1923. The maintenance of such burial grounds is undertaken against repayment by the Government concerned, and the cost is not met from the Commission's Endowment Fund. The work entailed is very small compared with the Commission's normal undertakings, but it has no doubt ensured, particularly where the Commission's personnel are on the spot, closer and more direct attention to these graves than was hitherto possible.

LINKS WITH THE RELATIVES

In this account it has been necessary to dwell, perhaps with some insistence, on the efficiency of administrative control and on the establishment of official contacts within the Commonwealth and outside. But by a happy inspiration the founders of the Commission provided a check against the too great absorption of the Commissioners in this essential part of their duties. It was largely due to their first Chairman, Lord Derby, that full advantage was taken of this provision.

The Charter, having named the official members, lays down that there shall also be appointed as members "such other persons, not exceeding the number of eight in all, as may from time to time be appointed members of the Commission by Royal Warrant under the Sign Manual of the Sovereign for the time being". Lord Derby was responsible for the initial selection of these eight unofficial members and resisted firmly the tendency to choose men representing official interests whose assistance it might be useful to enlist. He considered it more important to secure the services of

SOUTH AFRICAN NATIONAL MEMORIAL,
DELVILLE WOOD, FRANCE

NEWFOUNDLAND NATIONAL MEMORIAL,
BEAUMONT-HAMEL, FRANCE

15TH (SCOTTISH) DIVISION MEMORIAL, BUZANCY, FRANCE

Erected during the actual fighting in July, 1918, by the French 17th Division with the following inscription: "Ici fleurira toujours le glorieux chardon d'Ecosse parmi les roses de France".

1ST BATTALION SOUTH WALES BORDERERS MEMORIAL, GHELUVELT, BELGIUM

36TH (ULSTER) DIVISION MEMORIAL, THIEPVAL, FRANCE

MUNSTER MEMORIAL, YPRES

INDIAN MEMORIAL,
NEUVE-CHAPELLE, FRANCE

PORTSMOUTH NAVAL MEMORIAL

MEMORIAL TO THE MERCHANT NAVY AND FISHING FLEETS,
TOWER HILL, LONDON

NAME PANELS ON THE SOMME MEMORIAL,
THIEPVAL, FRANCE

MEMORIAL TABLET TO THE MILLION DEAD PLACED IN
CATHEDRALS IN FRANCE

men who would maintain constant touch with the relatives who were the natural guardians of the graves. For, to these relatives— by the wish of the Governments and peoples who entrusted the Commission with their task and by the tradition of individual rights and freedom which were the most cherished of their political possessions—the Commission were in the first place responsible.

Among those who have held appointments as unofficial members, and are now dead, were William Garstin, Rudyard Kipling, Harry Gosling and Robert Hudson. The two first of these lost their only sons in the War. Rudyard Kipling gave of his genius freely and whole-heartedly in the service of the commemoration of the dead; every inscription approved by the Commission was his in conception or in its final form, and his poem on the King's Pilgrimage in 1922 has a lasting place in the literature of our language.* It is owing to the presence and influence of men such as these in their councils that the Commission have never forgotten that their whole policy should be based on, and built up round, the sanctity both of the individual grave and of the name and memory of the man who has no known grave.

It would not be proper to conclude without a reference to the staff which has served under me in the twenty years now reviewed. A small part of it has been engaged in this work since the first years of the War; many passed from War service into that of the Commission, and having done their share in building the structure have gone to other work; some, engaged when the War was over, are still serving the Commission. These different elements have

---

* The place left vacant among the unofficial members by the death of Rudyard Kipling was accepted by his cousin, Mr Stanley Baldwin. At the same time, on the invitation of the Commission, Mr Edmund Blunden placed his services at their disposal, and he has attended meetings of the Commission when Mr Baldwin's duties as Prime Minister have prevented him from doing so.

worked in exceptional harmony, and without their sustained co-operation success would not have been possible; but it is neither that aspect of their work, nor the high level of ability which it was, after all, the Commission's duty to enlist, that is the most striking fact in retrospect.

My fellow-Commissioners, whose duties have called and still call them to watch many other spheres of human activity, would agree that the special nature of work in the Commission's service has engendered an exceptional type of zeal and personal devotion. It is this widespread devotion or fervour among the members of the Commission's staff in the conduct of their daily routine which has impressed most forcibly those who have controlled, and many who have observed, the work of the last twenty years.

The preservation of that spirit is as necessary as the durability of materials for the permanence of the work. It is a natural growth in those who have seen rising on the foundations, which they laid during the war, a monument worthy of their comrades-in-arms— men who fought

> "not for glory, nor for wealth, nor for honour, but for that freedom which no good man will surrender but with his life".

To transmit it to their successors they must have faith and vision—faith in their service as a living model of co-operation between the equal partner nations of the Commonwealth and vision that through their work Nation may speak peace unto Nation.

FABIAN WARE

LONDON
15 April 1937

THE MILLION DEAD

DISTRIBUTION OF CEMETERIES, GRAVES, AND MEMORIALS

Country	Number of dead buried in identified graves	Number of dead commemorated whose graves are not known	Total number of dead commemorated	War graves containing unidentified dead	Number of burial grounds containing war graves
EUROPE:					
Great Britain and Northern Ireland . .	88,174	39,375	127,549	457	9,262
Irish Free State .	2,525	2	2,527	27	550
France . . .	317,770	213,077	530,847	105,351	1,879
Belgium . . .	92,288	102,424	194,712	46,791	437
Ægean Islands . .	1,215	—	1,215	323	5
Austria . . .	6	—	6	3	4
Bulgaria . . .	212	—	212	3	5
Czechoslovakia . .	1	—	1	—	1
Danzig . . .	13	—	13	—	1
Denmark . .	53	—	53	12	20
Estonia . . .	15	—	15	—	2
Finland . . .	11	—	11	5	3
Gallipoli . .	8,968	26,883	35,851	13,503	31
Germany . .	6,535	25	6,560	38	25
Gibraltar . .	301	7	308	—	1
Greece . . .	8,689	2,801	11,490	596	17
Holland . . .	144	2	146	190	20
Hungary . . .	4	—	4	—	3
Italy . . .	3,364	427	3,791	57	91
Latvia . . .	32	—	32	4	1
Lithuania . .	2	—	2	—	1
Malta · . .	1,928	—	1,928	1	11
Norway . . .	80	—	80	86	42
Poland . . .	156	5	161	—	1
Portugal . . .	6	—	6	—	2

Country	Number of dead buried in identified graves	Number of dead commemorated whose graves are not known	Total number of dead commemorated	War graves containing unidentified dead	Number of burial grounds containing war graves
EUROPE (cont.):					
Rumania . . .	85	—	85	3	3
Russia . . .	362	190	552	18	11
Spain . . .	21	—	21	—	14
Sweden . . .	42	—	42	31	28
Switzerland . .	98	—	98	—	5
Turkey (excluding Gallipoli) . . .	147	—	147	—	4
Yugoslavia . .	156	—	156	9	3
ASIA:					
Aden . . .	141	619	760	—	4
Armenia . . .	1	—	1	—	1
Azerbaijan . .	47	—	47	7	2
British North Borneo	1	—	1	—	1
Ceylon . . .	83	—	83	—	17
China . . .	60	3	63	—	12
Cyprus . . .	29	—	29	—	5
Georgia . . .	101	—	101	10	3
Hong Kong . .	109	948	1,057	—	6
India . . .	3,711	15,836	19,547	—	169
Indo-China . .	1	—	1	—	1
Iran . . .	428	3,580	4,008	—	9
Iraq . . .	10,688	40,784	51,472	9,589	13
Japan . . .	1	—	1	—	1
Oman . . .	2	—	2	—	2
Palestine . . .	9,435	3,368	12,803	3,103	29
Philippine Islands .	1	—	1	—	1
Russia . . .	37	13	50	—	2
Straits Settlements .	64	—	64	—	6
Syria . . .	1,380	—	1,380	77	8
Turkey . . .	359	30	389	16	2
AUSTRALIA AND NEW ZEALAND:					
Australia . .	1,542	—	1,542	—	315

Country	Number of dead buried in identified graves	Number of dead com-memorated whose graves are not known	Total number of dead commemorated	War graves containing unidentified dead	Number of burial grounds containing war graves
AUSTRALIA AND NEW ZEALAND (cont.):					
Fiji . . .	4	—	4	—	1
Society Islands . .	2	—	2	—	1
New Britain and New Guinea . . .	32	—	32	—	5
New Zealand . .	1,565	169	1,734	—	308
Sandwich Islands .	1	—	1	—	1
NORTH AMERICA:					
Bermuda. . .	81	—	81	—	10
Canada . . .	6,503	300	6,803	—	1,697
Newfoundland . .	127	—	127	—	80
United States . .	309	—	309	—	247
SOUTH AND CENTRAL AMERICA:					
Argentina . .	2	—	2	—	2
Brazil · . .	12	—	12	—	3
British Guiana . .	11	—	11	—	5
British Honduras .	40	—	40	—	5
Chile . . .	4	—	4	—	4
Falkland Islands .	21	—	21	—	1
Guatemala . .	1	—	1	—	1
Panama Canal Zone .	3	—	3	—	1
Peru . . .	4	—	4	—	1
Uruguay . . .	3	—	3	—	1
WEST INDIES:					
Bahamas . . .	2	—	2	—	1
Barbados . . .	13	—	13	—	8
Cuba . . .	1	—	1	—	1
Jamaica . . .	165	—	165	—	13
Leeward Islands .	1	—	1	—	1
Trinidad . . .	7	—	7	—	3
Windward Islands .	43	—	43	—	6

Country	Number of dead buried in identified graves	Number of dead commemorated whose graves are not known	Total number of dead commemorated	War graves containing unidentified dead	Number of burial grounds containing war graves
AFRICA:					
Ascension Island .	6	—	6	—	1
Bechuanaland . .	1	—	1	—	1
Belgian Congo . .	1	—	1	—	1
Cape Verde Islands .	6	—	6	—	1
Egypt . . .	9,475	14,855	24,330	139	27
French North Africa .	51	—	51	—	13
French West Africa .	21	—	21	—	2
Gambia . . .	—	37	37	—	—
Gold Coast . .	11	770	781	—	4
Italian Somaliland .	2	1	3	—	2
Kenya . . .	600	43,638	44,238	39	13
Madeira . . .	3	—	3	—	1
Mauritius . .	30	—	30	—	8
Nigeria . . .	47	2,432	2,479	—	23
Northern Rhodesia .	25	1,571	1,596	—	2
Nyasaland . .	151	—	151	—	8
Portuguese East Africa	292	—	292	13	13
St Helena . .	5	—	5	—	1
Seychelles . .	49	289	338	—	1
Sierra Leone . .	159	1,117	1,276	—	2
Somaliland . .	2	111	113	—	1
South Africa . .	2,313	2	2,315	—	140
Southern Rhodesia .	43	66	109	—	9
South-West Africa .	378	—	378	—	23
Sudan . . .	72	—	72	—	6
Tanganyika . .	2,730	2,016	4,746	360	36
Uganda . . .	10	—	10	—	6
Zanzibar . . .	53	—	53	—	2
	587,117	517,773	1,104,890	180,861	15,846

THE MISSING

The following is a list of the Memorials to those officers and men who fell in the War, and who have no known grave.

Name of Memorial	Number commemorated
UNITED KINGDOM:	
Chatham Naval Memorial	8,541
Plymouth Naval Memorial	7,268
Portsmouth Naval Memorial	9,750
Tower Hill Memorial, London	12,674
Hollybrook Memorial, Southampton	1,857
FRANCE:	
Arras Memorial	35,925
Beaumont-Hamel (Newfoundland) Memorial	820
Caterpillar Valley (New Zealand) Memorial	1,273
Cambrai Memorial, Louverval	7,036
Cité Bonjean (New Zealand) Memorial, Armentières	48
Delville Wood Memorial (on behalf of the South African Memorial Committee)	
Grévillers (New Zealand)	455
La Ferté-sous-Jouarre Memorial	3,888
Le Touret Memorial	13,448
Loos Memorial	20,633
Marfaux (New Zealand) Memorial	10
Neuve-Chapelle (Indian) Memorial	4,847
Pozières Memorial	14,668
Noyelles-sur-Mer (Chinese) Memorial	46
"Salta" Memorial, Ste Marie Cemetery, Le Havre	144
Soissons Memorial	3,987
South African Native Labour Corps Memorial (Arques-la Bataille)	

Name of Memorial	Number commemorated
FRANCE (cont.):	
The Somme Memorial, Thiepval	73,367
V.C. Corner Australian Cemetery, Fromelles . .	1,299
*Villers-Bretonneux (Australian) Memorial . .	10,866
Vimy (Canadian) Memorial	11,285
Vis-en-Artois Memorial	9,903
BELGIUM:	
Buttes (New Zealand) Memorial	383
Menin Gate Memorial, Ypres	54,896
Messines Ridge (New Zealand) Memorial . . .	839
Nieuport Memorial	566
Ploegsteert Memorial	11,447
Tyne Cot Memorial, Passchendaele	34,957
Zeebrugge Memorial	4
ITALY:	
Giavera Memorial	154
Savona Memorial	274
GERMANY:	
Cologne Memorial	25
GIBRALTAR:	
Gibraltar Memorial, North Front Cemetery . .	7
POLAND:	
Posen Memorial	5
RUSSIA:	
Archangel Memorial	191
GREECE:	
Doiran Memorial	2,213
Mikra Memorial, Salonika . .	478
Monastir Road (Indian) Memorial .	163
TURKEY:	
Haidar Pasha Memorial, Constantinople	30

* Not yet completed.

Name of Memorial	Number commemorated
GALLIPOLI:	
Chunuk Bair (New Zealand) Memorial . .	856
Helles Memorial	20,752
Hill 60 (New Zealand) Memorial	183
Lone Pine Memorial	4,939
Twelve Tree Copse (New Zealand) Memorial . .	181
EGYPT:	
Chatby Memorial, Alexandria	983
Gizeh Memorial, Cairo	
Kantara Memorial	16
Port Tewfik (Indian) Memorial	4,928
PALESTINE:	
Jerusalem Memorial . . .	3,382
IRAN:	
Reshire British Memorial	219
*Reshire Indian Memorial	3,380
IRAQ:	
Basra Memorial . . .	41,048
ARABIA:	
Aden Memorial . .	627
INDIA:	
Bombay Memorial .	2,223
Delhi Memorial . .	13,516
Shillong Memorial .	95
CHINA:	
Hong Kong Memorial	947
EAST AFRICA:	
Dar es Salaam British and Indian Memorial . .	1,573
Dar es Salaam Native Memorial . . .	
Mombasa British Memorial	86
Mombasa Native Memorial	

* Not constructed.

Name of Memorial				Number commemorated
EAST AFRICA (cont.):				
Nairobi British and Indian Memorial	.	.	.	1,248
Nairobi Native Memorial	.	.	.	.	
Tanga (Jasin) Memorial	.	.	.	.	62
Tanga Memorial .	.	.	.	.	.	394
NIGERIA:				
Lagos Colonial Church Memorial	.	.	.	39
Lagos Memorial .	.	.	.	.	.	952
CANADA:				
Halifax Memorial, Nova Scotia	.	.	.	415
Victoria Memorial, British Columbia	.	.	.	41
NORTHERN RHODESIA:				
Abercorn (Native) Memorial .	.	.	.	1,467
GAMBIA:				
Bathurst Memorial	.	.	.	.	.	37
SIBERIA:				
Churkin Naval Cemetery Memorial, Vladivostok	.	13
SIERRA LEONE:				
Freetown (Native) Memorial .	.	.	.	1,136
SOMALILAND:				
Berbera Memorial	.	.	.	.	.	109
NEW ZEALAND:				
Canterbury Memorial	.	.	.	.	.	33
Auckland Memorial	.	.	.	.	.	40
Wellington Memorial	.	.	.	.	.	65
Otago Memorial .	.	.	.	.	.	31
SEYCHELLES:				
Mont-Fleuri Memorial, Victoria	.	.	.	289
BRITISH HONDURAS:				
Belize Memorial .	.	.	.	.	.	42
GOLD COAST:				
Accra Memorial .	.	.	.	.	64

APPENDICES A–E

APPENDIX A

NAMES OF COMMISSIONERS

President

H.R.H. the PRINCE OF WALES (1917–1936).
H.R.H. the DUKE OF YORK (1936).
H.R.H. the DUKE OF GLOUCESTER (1937–   ).

Chairman (Secretary of State for War)

The Rt Hon. the EARL OF DERBY (1917–1918).
The Rt Hon. the VISCOUNT MILNER (1918–1919).
The Rt Hon. WINSTON CHURCHILL (1919–1921).
The Rt Hon. SIR LAMING WORTHINGTON-EVANS (1921–1922).
The Rt Hon. the EARL OF DERBY (1922–1924).
The Rt Hon. STEPHEN WALSH (1924).
The Rt Hon. SIR LAMING WORTHINGTON-EVANS (1924–1929).
The Rt Hon. THOMAS SHAW (1929–1931).
The Most Hon. the MARQUESS OF CREWE (1931).
The Rt Hon. the VISCOUNT HAILSHAM (1931–1935).
The Rt Hon. the VISCOUNT HALIFAX (1935).
The Rt Hon. A. DUFF COOPER (1935–   ).

Vice-Chairman

Major-General SIR FABIAN WARE (1917–   ).

Secretary of State for the Colonies

The Rt Hon. W. H. LONG (1917–1919).
The Rt Hon. the VISCOUNT MILNER (1919–1921).
The Rt Hon. WINSTON CHURCHILL (1921–1922).
The Rt Hon. the DUKE OF DEVONSHIRE (1922–1924).
The Rt Hon. J. H. THOMAS (1924).
The Rt Hon. L. C. M. S. AMERY (1924–1929).

Secretary of State for the Colonies (cont.)

The Rt Hon. LORD PASSFIELD (1929–1931).
The Rt Hon. J. H. THOMAS (1931).
The Rt Hon. SIR PHILIP CUNLIFFE-LISTER (1931–1935).
The Rt Hon. MALCOLM MACDONALD (1935).
The Rt Hon. J. H. THOMAS (1935–1936).
The Rt Hon. W. G. A. ORMSBY-GORE (1936–   ).

Secretary of State for India

The Rt Hon. E. S. MONTAGU (1917–1922).
The Rt Hon. the VISCOUNT PEEL (1922–1924).
The Rt Hon. SIR S. OLIVIER (1924).
The Rt Hon. the EARL OF BIRKENHEAD (1924–1928).
The Rt Hon. the VISCOUNT PEEL (1928–1929).
The Rt Hon. W. WEDGWOOD BENN (1929–1931).
The Rt Hon. SIR SAMUEL HOARE (1931–1935).
The Most Hon. the MARQUESS OF ZETLAND (1935–   ).

First Commissioner of Works

The Rt Hon. SIR ALFRED MOND (1917–1921).
The Rt Hon. the EARL OF CRAWFORD AND BALCARRES
    (1921–1922).
The Rt Hon. SIR JOHN BAIRD (1922–1924).
The Rt Hon. F. W. JOWETT (1924).
The Rt Hon. the VISCOUNT PEEL (1924–1928).
The Most Hon. the MARQUESS OF LONDONDERRY (1928–1929).
The Rt Hon. GEORGE LANSBURY (1929–1931).
The Most Hon. the MARQUESS OF LONDONDERRY (1931).
The Rt Hon. W. G. A. ORMSBY-GORE (1931–1936).
The Rt Hon. the EARL STANHOPE (1936–   ).

Dominion of Canada

The Hon. SIR GEORGE PERLEY (1917–1922).
The Hon. PETER C. LARKIN (1922–1930).
The Hon. G. H. FERGUSON (1930–1935).
The Hon. VINCENT MASSEY (1935–   ).

Commonwealth of Australia

The Rt Hon. ANDREW FISHER (1917–1921).
The Rt Hon. SIR JOSEPH COOK (1921–1927).
Major-General the Hon. SIR GRANVILLE DE LAUNE RYRIE
(1927–1932).
The Rt Hon. S. M. BRUCE (1932–   ).

Dominion of New Zealand

The Hon. SIR THOMAS MACKENZIE (1917–1920).
Colonel the Hon. SIR JAMES ALLEN (1920–1926).
The Hon. SIR JAMES PARR (1926–1929).
SIR THOMAS WILFORD (1929–1933).
The Hon. SIR JAMES PARR (1934–1936).
Mr W. J. JORDAN (1936–   ).

Union of South Africa

The Rt Hon. W. P. SCHREINER (1917–1919).
The Hon. SIR EDGAR WALTON (1920–1924).
Mr J. S. SMIT (1925–1929).
Mr C. T. TE WATER (1929–   ).

Newfoundland

Dr E. F. S. GREEN (1917–1918).
The Hon. SIR EDGAR BOWRING (1918–1923).
Lieut.-Colonel T. NANGLE (1923–1924).
Captain VICTOR GORDON (1924–1928).
The Hon. SIR JOHN R. BENNETT (1928).
Mr D. J. DAVIES (1928–1933).
The Hon. SIR EDGAR BOWRING (1933–   ).

Unofficial Members

SIR WILLIAM GARSTIN (1917–1925).
Mr HARRY GOSLING (1917–1930).
Mr RUDYARD KIPLING (1917–1936).
Lieut.-General SIR NEVIL MACREADY (1917–1921).
Admiral SIR EDMUND S. POE (1917–1921).

Unofficial Members (cont.)

General Sir Herbert C. O. Plumer (1917–1920).
Major-General Sir Fabian Ware (1917–   ).
Lieut.-General Sir George Macdonogh (1920–   ).
Sir Robert Hudson (1920–1927).
Vice-Admiral Sir Morgan Singer (1921–   ).
Sir H. Maddocks (1921–1931).
Lieut.-General Sir Robert D. Whigham (1923–1927).
General Sir Walter Braithwaite (1927–1931).
Lord Stanley (1928–   ).
Mr J. J. Lawson (1931–   ).
General Sir Archibald Montgomery-Massingberd (1931–1933).
Mr W. P. Spens (1931–   ).
General Sir Cecil F. Romer (1933–1935).
Lieut.-General Sir Harry Knox (1935–   ).
The Rt Hon. Stanley Baldwin (1936–   ).

APPENDIX B

ADMINISTRATION

VICE-CHAIRMAN
Major-General Sir Fabian Ware (1917–   ).

ADMINISTRATIVE HEADS OF BRANCHES

Finance   Lieut.-Colonel Sir Herbert Ellissen (1918–1927).
Lieut.-Colonel C. P. Oswald (1927–   ).

Works   Lieut.-Colonel F. R. Durham (1919–1926).
Lieut.-Colonel H. F. Robinson (1926–   ).

Records   Major H. F. Chettle (1919–   ).

Secretarial   J. E. Talbot, Esq. (1917–1919).
Colonel Lord Arthur Browne (1919–1931).

Legal   Major C. K. Phillips (1919–1925).
Captain H. P. R. Foster (1925–   ).

EUROPEAN DISTRICT
(France, Belgium, Germany, Italy, etc.)
Colonel H. T. Goodland (1919–1928).
Lieut.-Colonel F. Higginson (1928–   ).

EASTERN DISTRICT
(Egypt, Palestine, Macedonia, Gallipoli, Iraq, etc.)
Lieut.-Colonel C. E. Hughes (1919–1936).
Brig.-General Sir Herbert Hart (1936–   ).

CANADA
Colonel H. C. Osborne (1920–   ).

SOUTH AFRICA
Captain J. G. Marais (1925–   ).

APPENDIX C

On 11 November 1918, the higher appointments in the Directorate of Graves Registration and Enquiries were as follows:

Director-General of Graves Registration and Enquiries: Maj. Gen. F. A. G. WARE, C.M.G.

Assistant Adjutant General: Bt. Lt.-Col. G. H. STOBART, D.S.O.

Deputy Assistant Adjutant General: Maj. J. R. N. Viscount STOPFORD.

Deputy Director of Graves Registration and Enquiries (France): Lt.-Col. G. O. CORNOCK TAYLOR.

Assistant Director-General of Graves Registration and Enquiries (France): Lt.-Col. A. A. MESSER, D.S.O.

Deputy Assistant Director-General of Graves Registration and Enquiries (Egypt): Maj. W. W. T. MASSIAH PALMER.

Upon the cessation of hostilities the Directorate was entrusted with the task of searching the former battlefields and of transferring to recognised cemeteries the bodies of those buried in isolated graves, as well as of maintaining the cemeteries until such time as they could be handed over to the Imperial War Graves Commission for permanent construction. To cope with this work, the establishment of the Directorate was increased, but, owing to the rapid progress of demobilisation, there were constant changes in the personnel. Among the senior officers who rendered valuable service in the Directorate between 1918 and March 1921, the following may be mentioned:

Brig.-Gen. E. S. BURDER; Brig.-Gen. A. G. P. McNALTY; Brig.-Gen. L. J. WYATT; Lt.-Col. K. J. DICK-CUNYNGHAM; Lt. Col. J. M. MITCHELL; Lt. Col. P. B. AKROYD; Lt.-Col. H. G. B. ·MILLER; Col. S. J. MURRAY; Lt.-Col. E. A. S. GELL; and Dame ADELAIDE LIVINGSTONE, who did work of great value in searching for the missing in France and in Germany.

APPENDIX D

THE ANGLO-GERMAN-FRENCH MIXED COMMITTEE

(ORIGINAL MEMBERSHIP)

BRITISH

Honorary Members

His Excellency the Rt. Hon. Sir ERIC PHIPPS, G.C.M.G., C.V.O. (the British Ambassador in Berlin).

Marshal of the Royal Air Force Viscount TRENCHARD, G.C.B., G.C.V.O., D.S.O.

Members

Sir FABIAN WARE, K.C.V.O., K.B.E., C.B., C.M.G.

Sir EDWARD PEACOCK, G.C.V.O.

Lieut.-General Sir GEORGE MACDONOGH, G.B.E., K.C.B., K.C.M.G.

J. J. LAWSON, Esq., M.P.

GERMAN

Honorary Members

His Excellency HERR LEOPOLD VON HOESCH (the German Ambassador in London).

Generaloberst VON SEECKT.

Members

Ministerialdirektor Dr FRIEDRICH GAUS.

Legationsrat GUSTAV RÖDIGER.

Geheimer Oberregierungsrat HORNING.

Dr S. E. EULEN.

FRENCH

Honorary Member

His Excellency M. ANDRÉ FRANÇOIS-PONCET (the French Ambassador in Berlin).

Member

Intendant-Général P. D. VINCENSINI, K.B.E.

Secretary-General

Major H. F. CHETTLE, C.M.G., O.B.E.

APPENDIX E

NATIONAL BATTLEFIELDS MEMORIAL COMMITTEE

(1919-1921)

Chairman

The Rt Hon. the EARL OF MIDLETON, K.P.

Members

Colonel the Hon. SIR JAMES ALLEN, K.C.B. (New Zealand).
The Rt Hon. G. N. BARNES, M.P.
Rear-Admiral SIR R. W. BENTINCK, K.C.M.G.
SIR R. A. BLANKENBERG, K.B.E. (South Africa).
SIR LIONEL EARLE, K.C.B., K.C.V.O., C.M.G.
The Rt Hon. A. FISHER (Australia).
Mr D. S. MacCOLL, M.A., LL.D.
Lieut.-General SIR G. M. W. MACDONOGH, K.C.B., K.C.M.G.
    (Adjutant-General).
Lieut.-Colonel T. NANGLE (Newfoundland).
The Hon. SIR GEORGE PERLEY, K.C.M.G. (Canada).
SIR M. G. RAMSAY, K.C.B. (The Treasury).
The Rt Hon. the LORD RIDDELL.
Mr J. S. SARGENT, R.A.
Major-General the Rt Hon. J. E. B. SEELY, C.B., C.M.G., D.S.O.,
    M.P.
SIR ASTON WEBB, K.C.V.O., C.B., P.R.A.

Secretary

Mr K. LYON, O.B.E. (The War Office).

THE SILENT CITIES

AN ILLUSTRATED GUIDE TO THE WAR CEMETERIES AND MEMORIALS TO THE
MISSING IN FRANCE & FLANDERS 1914-1918

by Sidney C. Hurst

N&MPress. xv + 407pp with 959 b/w illus and 31 maps

ISBN: 9781843422624

The Silent Cities was Rudyard Kipling's inspired name for the Cemeteries
of the Western Front and this book, with the aid of maps, illustrations and
descriptive notes, sets out to provide a complete guide to all Cemeteries
containing war graves and all Memorials recording the Missing of the
Forces of the British Empire who fell in France and Flanders during the
Great War. The index lists no less than 2,485 which are identified on the
maps. These maps divide the book into geographical sections, and each
section contains b/w illustrations and descriptions of those Cemeteries and
Memorials, within the limits of the map, that record more tha 40 British
Dead. The numbers of other nationalities, e.g. Germans, French, buried in
the Cemetery are also given. Some contain 'Special Memorials' indicating
officers and men whose graves have been destroyed by shell-fire or who
are known or believed to be buried in that Cemetery. This is an essential
vade mecum for any visit to the Western Front.

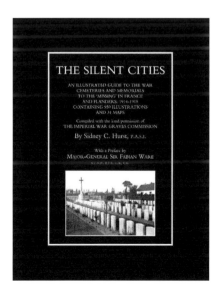

www.naval-military-press.com